At the Construction Site

Look, a Dump Truck!

By Julia Jaske

A dump truck can carry dirt.

A dump truck can dump dirt.

A dump truck can carry soil.

A dump truck can dump soil.

A dump truck can carry
small rocks.

A dump truck can dump
small rocks.

A dump truck can carry big rocks.

A dump truck can dump big rocks.

 A dump truck can carry sand.

A dump truck can dump sand.

 A dump truck can carry gravel.

A dump truck can dump gravel.

Word List

truck
carry
dirt
dump
soil
small
rocks
big
sand
gravel

76 Words

A dump truck can carry dirt.
A dump truck can dump dirt.
A dump truck can carry soil.
A dump truck can dump soil.
A dump truck can carry small rocks.
A dump truck can dump small rocks.
A dump truck can carry big rocks.
A dump truck can dump big rocks.
A dump truck can carry sand.
A dump truck can dump sand.
A dump truck can carry gravel.
A dump truck can dump gravel.

Published in the United States of America by Cherry Lake Publishing Group
Ann Arbor, Michigan
www.cherrylakepublishing.com

Photo Credits: © Creativa Images/Shutterstock, cover, 1, 14; © zhengchengbao/Shutterstock, back cover; © Mr. Tempter/Shutterstock, 2; © nurkhann/Shutterstock, 3; © Vladimir Mulder/Shutterstock, 4; © PetraMenclovaCZ/Shutterstock, 5; © erlucho/Shutterstock, 6; © jacquesdurocher/istock, 7; © Salienko Evgenii/Shutterstock, 8; © Mr. Tempter/Shutterstock, 9; © Maksim Safaniuk/istock, 10; © DedMityay/istock, 11; © Baxternator/istock, 12; © Dreamsquare/Shutterstock, 13

Cherry Blossom Press is an imprint of Cherry Lake Publishing Group.

Library of Congress Cataloging-in-Publication Data

Names: Jaske, Julia, author.
Title: Look, a dump truck! / by Julia Jaske.
Description: Ann Arbor, Michigan : Cherry Lake Publishing, [2021] | Series: At the Construction Site
Identifiers: LCCN 2021007839 (print) | LCCN 2021007840 (ebook) | ISBN 9781534188167 (Paperback) | ISBN 9781534189560 (PDF) | ISBN 9781534190962 (eBook)
Subjects: LCSH: Dump trucks–Juvenile literature. | Illustrated children's books.
Classification: LCC TL230.15 .J37 2021 (print) | LCC TL230.15 (ebook) | DDC 629.224–dc23
LC record available at https://lccn.loc.gov/2021007839
LC ebook record available at https://lccn.loc.gov/2021007840

Printed in the United States of America
Corporate Graphics